D1569769

A BEACON ★ BIOGRAPHY

Brie LARSON

John Bankston

PURPLE TOAD
PUBLISHING

PURPLE TOAD
PUBLISHING

Printing   1   2   3   4   5   6   7   8   9

A Beacon Biography

Alexandria Ocasio-Cortez
Angelina Jolie
Anthony Davis
Ben Simmons
Big Time Rush
Bill Nye
Brie Larson
Bryce Harper
Cam Newton
Carly Rae Jepsen
Carson Wentz
Chadwick Boseman
Daisy Ridley
Drake
Ed Sheeran

Ellen DeGeneres
Elon Musk
Ezekiel Elliott
Gal Gadot
Harry Styles of One Direction
Jennifer Lawrence
Joel Embiid
John Boyega
Keanu Reeves
Kevin Durant
Lorde
Malala
Markus "Notch" Persson,
   Creator of Minecraft
Megan Rapinoe

Meghan Markle
Michelle Obama
Millie Bobby Brown
Misty Copeland
Mo'ne Davis
Muhammad Ali
Neil deGrasse Tyson
Oprah Winfrey
Peyton Manning
Robert Griffin III (RG3)
Scarlett Johansson
Stephen Colbert
Stephen Curry
Tom Holland
Zendaya

Library of Congress Cataloging-in-Publication Data
Bankston, John
   Brie Larson / Written by: John Bankston
      p.cm.
Includes bibliographic references, glossary, and index.
ISBN 9781624695148-
1. Larson, Brie, 1989—Juvenile literature. 2. Motion picture actors and actresses—United States—Biographies—Juvenile literature. Series: I. A Beacon Biography.

PN2287.L2846 B36 2019
791.4302/8092 B

Library of Congress Control Number: 2019949377

eBook ISBN: 9781624695155

ABOUT THE AUTHOR: John Bankston is the author of over 150 books for young readers, including biographies of Emma Stone, Jennifer Lawrence, and Jodie Foster. A member of SAG-AFTRA (the actor's union), he played the Town Crier, a recurring role on local Boston TV show *Willie Whistle*, when he was a toddler. Since then he has appeared in dozens of plays, short films, and low-budget movies. He has had feature roles in the movie *I Now Pronounce You Chuck and Larry* and the TV shows *Sabrina the Teenage Witch* and *Jericho*. He can briefly be seen as a reporter in *Iron Man*. Today he lives in Miami Beach, Florida with his ChiJack, Astronaut.

CONTENTS

The Right Role

Brie celebrates the U.S. Air Force's 71st birthday by screening the first footage of Captain Marvel with fans at the National Air and Space Museum, Smithsonian Institution.

Brie Larson couldn't believe she was crying. The movie she was watching wasn't supposed to be sad. It was *Wonder Woman*, a superhero movie. Unfortunately, the company she worked for, Marvel Studios, wasn't the one who'd made it.

In 2008, the movie *Iron Man* launched the Marvel Cinematic Universe. MCU is a movie world in which a superhero team called the Avengers battles for peace.

In 2017, *Wonder Woman* was released. Like Batman and Superman, this movie was part of DC Comics, not Marvel. *Wonder Woman* made over $800 million across the world.

Larson was one of many who saw it. "As a kid, I wanted to be an adventurer . . . ," she said. "I wanted to get my hands dirty. But it wasn't until being in the theater seeing *Wonder Woman* . . . I was like, 'Why is this making me cry so much?' " Although she had played many strong and independent characters, she'd never had that chance in a superhero movie.[1]

Then, in 2016, she was given her chance. She was asked to play Carol Danvers, who starts off as Captain Marvel's girlfriend but later

Marvel mastermind Kevin Feige thought Brie was perfect to play Captain Marvel, a tough, smart fighter pilot who becomes a superhero.

becomes the superhero herself. Danvers shows up in the comics in 1968, but in the 1970s and 1980s, Marvel Comics wanted more girls to read their stories. They created Spider-Woman and She-Hulk—and they made Carol Danvers Ms. Marvel.

In those days, most female superheroes wore bikinis, even when they were fighting evildoers or flying an invisible plane. Brie noticed this clothing trend when she visited Marvel Studios. There was a wall of superhero posters. "If you look at the comics, the further you go back, the less clothes Carol Danvers seems to be wearing . . . ," Marvel Studios President Kevin Feige explained. "Brie pointed it out on the wall, and we went, 'Yeah . . . just so you know, that's not what we're doing.' She goes, 'OK. I didn't think so, but I'm glad you said that.' "[2]

Instead, Danvers would be a fighter pilot in the 1990s. Even in that decade, women were not permitted to fly in combat missions. Brie trained for the role by going up in a real fighter jet. She also lifted weights for four hours a day. Soon she could lift twice as much as she weighed. She became so strong, she could push her trainer's jeep up a hill!

Today the Disney Company owns Marvel. Almost twenty years earlier, Brie had starred in a Disney Channel movie called *Right on Track*. She and costar Beverley Mitchell played sisters Courtney and

Erica Enders. In real life the sisters were racecar drivers. Erica was eight years old when she and her sister started in the National Hot Rod Association Junior Dragster division in the 1990s. They won two National Championships. In the movie, they did the racing stunts for Brie and Beverley. *The Hollywood Reporter* said the movie was "loaded with energetic racing scenes, even if it's a bit corny around the edges." It also called Beverley and Brie "lively."[3]

In the 1990s, Disney's *All-New Mickey Mouse Club* introduced future stars Britney Spears, Justin Timberlake, Christina Aguilera, and Ryan Gosling. Miley Cyrus and Selena Gomez became famous on Disney Channel shows in the 2000s. Today, Zendaya, Dove Cameron, Stefanie Scott, and Debby Ryan star in movies. They also got their big break on the Disney Channel. Yet after *Right on Track*, Brie wasn't interested in staying with Disney.

"I just couldn't do it. I always had this attraction to holding up a mirror to the world, and this didn't feel like real life," Brie explained. "I wondered what would be the point."[4]

Instead, Brie took acting jobs that meant something to her. Sometimes she didn't have much money. Sometimes she didn't work for months. It would take twenty years before she played a superhero—and again worked for Disney. Her adventure began when she was a shy girl telling her mother she wanted to act.

At San Diego Comic-Con International in 2016, Brie answered questions during a panel discussion after announcing her role as Captain Marvel.

Chapter

2

The California capital may seem an unlikely birthplace for a future star, but Sacramento was close to San Francisco's world-class theaters and performance schools.

Struggle

Brie was born on October 1, 1989. She lived in Sacramento, the capital of California. When she was born her name was Brianne Sidonie Desaulniers. Her parents were Heather Edwards and Sylvain Desaulniers. They were both chiropractors, helping people who suffer from back pain. They worked from home. Home was also where Brie and her younger sister Milaine went to school.

Heather was born in California. She was Welsh, English, Swedish, German, and Scottish. Sylvain was French-Canadian. Brie spoke French before she spoke English.

Young people often dream about what they will do when they grow up. Maybe they will fight fires. Or maybe they will want to help animals. Brie remembers the day she told her mom what she wanted to do for the rest of her life. She was six years old.

"I was just so painfully shy. I couldn't make eye contact," Brie remembered. She had gone into the kitchen, telling her mom, "while she was doing the dishes, that I wanted to be an actor. She was just floored and . . . thought that surely I was repeating something that I had heard someone else say. My mom says that I just wouldn't shut up

The Geary Theater at San Francisco's American Conservatory Theater has welcomed legends like Sarah Bernhardt, Clark Gable, and Boris Karloff onto its stage. It also enrolled Brie into its school—the youngest performer in its history.

about it and just kept saying, 'I really want to take acting lessons.' And so she agreed."[1]

They made a deal. Brie would take lessons once a week. After a year, her parents would help her take the next step. Long before the year was up, Brie was in local plays. She also traveled to San Francisco, becoming the American Conservatory Theater's youngest student. Her mother then took a huge risk.

She packed Brie and Milaine into a car and drove south to Los Angeles. They moved into the Oakwood Apartments, a short-term home for young actors hoping for their big break. It is also across the street from Warner Brothers, a studio lot where shows like *Gilmore Girls* and *Pretty Little Liars* were filmed.

Dating to 1928, the Warner Brothers studio lot in Burbank, California has been the site for filming movies such as The Maltese Falcon, Rebel Without a Cause, *and* Harry Potter and the Chamber of Secrets. *TV shows have also been filmed there, including* Pretty Little Liars *and* Gilmore Girls. *It is just across the street from Brie's first home in Los Angeles.*

"It was all one room; the bed came out of the wall," Brie remembered. When the bed was down, there was very little space. Sometimes they pretended it was a trampoline. "I had two pairs of jeans, a couple shirts, a couple headbands and a pair of orange Converse [sneakers]. My mom created this amazing world, and I never remembered it as being a time where things were tight, and we were just eating Top Ramen and 99-cent Jack in the Box tacos, and I didn't have any toys."[2]

One night she awoke to her mother crying. "She was holding her hand over her mouth, trying not to wake us up . . . ," Brie remembered. "Years later, I realized that right before we had left for what was supposed to be a three-week thing, my dad said he wanted a divorce."[3]

Brie didn't see her father much after the move. As an adult, she admits she's pretty much forgotten how to speak French.

Soon after the move, Brie started auditioning. She went to offices and read lines from a TV show or movie. "The smallest fraction of a thing gets you cut, and if you have any sort of sense, you realize how impossible the situation is," she said. "Sometimes after getting knocked down a million times you think, 'Oh my [gosh], I'm done.' "[4]

She memorized monologues. New actors recite these long speeches for agents. Agents help them get work. Brie memorized the entire Shel Silverstein poem, "Sarah Cynthia Sylvia Stout Would Not Take the Garbage Out!"

Brie admits, "I was incredibly serious. I wanted to be taken seriously." Over twenty years later, she still remembers her first audition. It was for a fish stick ad.

Ten young actors lined up in a room. Each was asked what they liked. The others said things like ice cream and friends and soccer. Then, she was asked, "Brianne, what do you like to do?" She replied, "I like to act." "But what else?" she was asked. "Do you have any hobbies?" "No. I like to act."

"I felt so upset that they didn't ask me about my monologue," she later admitted. Her mom was waiting on the other side of the door "and I burst through, sobbing, 'They didn't ask me about my monologue!' I cried for a while about that."[5]

No matter how old they are, most actors start small. Many work as extras. This means they stand behind the stars, filling a scene by pretending to eat or talk. Brie did this for a while, standing in a room talking or making other sounds. No matter how hard she tried, she could not get a speaking part on a TV show or in a movie. Brie had been in Los Angeles for almost two years. She was ready to give up. Then the nine-year-old got to act on a show that would air long after her bedtime.

Today Brie is known as a world famous, award-winning actress, but she struggled for over twenty years before making it big.

At Captain Marvel's *premiere, Brie sported a dress and earrings with repeating stars—a nod to the superhero she plays.*

More than One Break

In 1998, *The Tonight Show with Jay Leno* was the most popular program on late night shows that air after 11:00 p.m. Besides talking to famous people, Jay Leno had funny bits. One group of bits was made-up ads.

Although Brie couldn't get a job on a real commercial, she acted in over a dozen fake ones. On *The Tonight Show* she played a girl who loved her Roadkill Easy Bake Oven, her Malibu Mudslide Barbie, and other fake products. She got to meet Jay Leno, but she was more excited to meet the actor who played Jack in the real Jack in the Box commercials.

Appearing on the fake ads wasn't just about getting seen by the millions of people who watched *The Tonight Show*. People who help choose actors for movies, TV shows, and commercials are called casting directors. They also watch *The Tonight Show*. In 1998 and 1999, they began to ask about the funny blond girl who pretended to be a Girl Scout. They started giving her parts.

Besides playing a dad on Full House, Bob Saget played Brie's father on Raising Dad.

Brie began acting in several TV shows. She was in an episode of *Popular* and the hit show *Touched by an Angel.* She also had parts in the movies *Special Delivery* and *Madison.* When she was 11 years old, she was cast in the TV show *Raising Dad.* The show starred Bob Saget. He was well known as the dad in *Full House.* In the new show, Brie played his daughter. Kat Dennings played her sister. The two would become friends, and Kat would go on to star in *2 Broke Girls* and *Thor.* Brie's other jobs had lasted only one or two weeks. This one could last for years.

Unfortunately, *Raising Dad* was canceled. Still, it was a good experience for Brie. It was where she met her music manager. The manager had heard her playing backstage. Soon she was working with producers who helped her record an album. "Invisible Girl," Brie's song about not getting a part in the play *Peter Pan,* was played on L.A.'s top radio station

Long before they joined the Marvel Cinematic Universe, Kat Dennings and Brie were costars on Raising Dad.

KISS-FM. Her album, *Finally Out of P.E.*, was released in 2005. She went on tour, opening for actor-singer Jesse McCartney. Although she enjoyed playing live, his fans were not as interested in her music. Brie's album sold only a few thousand copies. Besides poor album sales, Brie didn't get to write most of her songs and didn't like the ones that were written for her.

Exploring her musical side led to Brie opening for Jesse McCartney.

Brie became frustrated because for ten years she mainly played small parts in TV shows and movies.

Brie often played mean girls in movies. In *Sleepover*, she played one of the popular girls trying to win a scavenger hunt. The movie starred Mika Boorem and Alexa Vega. Their characters hoped winning the hunt would earn them a lunch table by the fountain instead of by the dumpster. Brie was also in *13 Going on 30*. Her credit? "One of the Six Chicks." Future *Pretty Little Liars* star Ashley Benson was also one of the "Six."

*Amber Heard, Brie's costar in **Remember the Daze,** played a super-hero first—starring with Jason Momoa in 2018's **Aquaman.***

Brie kept doing single episodes of TV shows. She appeared in *Hope and Faith* and *The Ghost Whisperer*. In the movie *Remember the Daze*, she played a teen girl who never leaves her room while her sister has adventures. She also starred in *Hoot*, a movie about teens fighting to save owls in Florida.

Unfortunately the jobs she had on TV shows did not last long. Few people saw her. Most of the movies she was in did not make much money.

That changed when she was cast in the Showtime series *United States of Tara*. Toni Collette plays Tara, and Brie plays her daughter. She starred in 36 episodes over three years. When the show ended in

2011, Brie was no longer a teenager. She was in her 20s and had been acting for more than half her life. Most of that time, she had been worried about money. Sometimes she barely had enough to eat.

She was so broke, she took a small part in a big movie. Usually she didn't like playing the girlfriend. Brie found it boring. But she would make more money from this job than she had ever made before.

Toni Collette has won awards and starred in movies but is probably best known for playing the mother in 1999's The Sixth Sense.

In 2016, Brie accepted the Academy Award for Best Actress in a Motion Picture for Room —*a movie in which she never thought she'd get a part.*

Long before playing a pirate, Johnny Depp played a cop pretending to be a teen on the TV series *21 Jump Street*. Twenty-one years after the show ended, a movie was made that was based on the show. It would star Jonah Hill and Channing Tatum as undercover teenagers. Unlike the TV show, the movie was meant to be funny. Tatum was in his 30s when he played the high school student.

At 22, Brie still looked like a teen. She had been homeschooled, but she liked pretending to be in high school. "I never thought that I missed out on anything," she admitted. "I wasn't interested in going to the school dances. I wasn't interested in going to the football games. What I wanted was to be in my room painting my walls and doing weird stuff."[1]

Brie finally had an easy time getting the job playing Jonah Hill's girlfriend Molly. Hill had introduced her to "these two young guys who had pads of paper in their hands and plaid shirts on. I was like, 'Who are these young kids?' . . . One of them gave me a stick of gum." When she auditioned for *21 Jump Street*, she realized these friends were the directors. "It was one of the best auditions I ever had. I'm not saying I even did an amazing job, but by the end of it I was going on vacation with them, we were going to make long-sleeve Hawaiian shirts."[2]

The movie did very well. It cost $40 million to make but earned over $200 million. Nearly everyone who saw it liked its mix of comedy and action.[3] Many also liked how Brie played a brave young woman who makes her own choices.

After being funny, Brie turned serious. *Short Term 12* is about a woman working at a home for troubled teens. After a teen girl arrives at the facility, she helps Brie's character remember bad things that had happened to her.

Brie auditioned online. She told the director she'd applied for a job doing the same kind of work as the character. She believed the job would help her act. She didn't get the job, but she did get the part.

Short Term 12 won several awards, but few saw the movie. One of those who did was Emma Donoghue, an Irish-Canadian writer. She was writing the movie version of her novel *Room*. It tells the story of a woman who spent seven years with her son living in a shed after she was kidnapped. It describes their escape and life afterward.

Many actresses wanted the role of the mother in *Room*. "I was told about the book, and I read it and loved it," Brie explained. "And I thought, 'This is an amazing part, and I will never get to play it.'"[4]

She was wrong. The author and movie's director agreed that Brie was perfect for the part. They did not realize how perfect. The room in *Room* reminded Brie of her first tiny L.A. apartment.

After getting the job, she worked very hard. She lost weight and stayed out of the sun. She wanted to look like someone who had been indoors for a long time, without enough to eat.

Off camera, Brie spent time with Jacob Tremblay, the actor who played her son. "I remembered the times that I was talked to like a person and the times that I was talked to like a kid," she explained about her childhood. Brie treated Jacob as her equal.[5]

Room won awards—and so did Brie. She won the Golden Globe Award for Best Actress in a Motion Picture. She won the Screen Actors Guild Award. And she won the biggest movie award: the Oscar.

She enjoyed the awards, but going to the ceremonies made her nervous. "Getting dressed up, going to events . . . ," she explained. "That's the part that has always terrified me. You can see dozens of photos where I have zero hair and makeup and I'm wearing my own jeans and T-shirt, because I was not that interested in that side of it."[6]

Despite starring in movies and winning awards, Brie lived a quiet life. Most people did not know who she was when she got coffee or went shopping. That was about to change.

Brie shared the spotlight with fellow Oscar winners Mark Rylance, Leonardo DiCaprio, and Alicia Vikander.

Brie stands tall with her Marvel cast, including **Spider-Man** stars Tom Holland and Zendaya.

Winning the Oscar changed Brie's life. She started getting jobs without auditioning. She got a lead role in the blockbuster *Kong: Skull Island*, where she played reporter Mason Weaver.

Brie no longer had to worry about money, but instead of buying a fancy car or a big house, Brie bought . . . new underwear! "To me, that's a luxury item," she admitted. "I took photos of the bag."[1]

The movie gave her a new best friend: actor Samuel L. Jackson. He had been a star for almost as long as Brie was alive. He did not just give her advice. He helped make one of her dreams come true.

Brie had started making short films in her tweens. She wrote them, filmed them, and starred in them. "I had a disco ball that I would put in front of the door of the garage—so if the light was on it meant we were filming. This way no one would come in and ruin the movie," she said.[2]

She liked using a camera. In 2017, she directed her first movie. Being a director is different from being an actor. Actors mainly worry about the job they do. Directors worry about many different jobs. The way a movie looks and sounds has a lot to do with the director.

When she isn't accepting awards or playing a superhero, Brie likes to dress light and casual, as she does during an appearance at San Diego's Comic-Con International.

One of her first jobs as director was casting Jackson in her movie *Unicorn Store*. He plays a man who runs a mysterious shop. Brie plays Kit. When she visits his store, he promises her a real live unicorn, but first she has to build it a home and do other things to get ready. The movie is a blend of a small child's dreams and an adult's problems. Not everyone liked it. Although it was made in 2017, most people did not see it until it came out on Netflix two years later.

By this time, Brie was already starring in the movie that would make her famous across the world.

MCU movies have three things in common. They each cost over $100 million to make. They earned around $1 *billion* around the world. And until 2018, they all starred a white male.

That changed with *Black Panther*, the first MCU movie to star a black man. Some thought that people overseas would not want to see *Black Panther*. They were mistaken. The movie made over $1.3 billion, and almost half of that came from outside the U.S.[3]

Yet none of the 20 MCU movies starred a woman. Marvel President Kevin Feige explained, "There were a lot of men in [the]Avengers."[4]

Feige encouraged Brie to star in *Captain Marvel*. When she accepted the part, she did more than star in the movie. She insisted that women and people of color get jobs working on it. She also spoke out about how most of the reporters she met were men.

Some were upset by what she said. They wanted *Captain Marvel* to fail. The website Rotten Tomatoes offers reviews from both professional critics and casual viewers. It lets people know how popular a movie or TV show is. The site also tracked how many people wanted to see a movie before it came out. With *Captain Marvel*, however, people who were mad at Brie flooded the site, saying they did not want to see the movie. Eventually, Rotten Tomatoes removed the feature.

Fans around the world are now dressing as their new favorite superhero, Captain Marvel.

Brie knew if the movie failed, some would blame her. There might be fewer movies starring women. If it did well, she would be more famous than she'd ever been before.

Across the world, *Captain Marvel* made over $1 billion. There were Captain Marvel toys that looked like her. Her face was on magazine covers. She was even on a toothbrush!

Six weeks after the premiere of *Captain Marvel*, *Avengers: Endgame* was released. The last film in the series, it stars a diverse cast, including Brie Larson. It would make the most money of any MCU movie.

When she spoke about the first MCU movie to star a female superhero, Larson could have been talking about herself. "Change is scary," she said, "and it takes time for it to come. It's slow but it's happening."[5]

It seems both MCU fans and Brie Larson have embraced change.

1989   Brianne Sidonie Desaulniers is born on October 1 in Sacramento, California, to Heather Edwards and Sylvain Desaulniers. Brie will late take the last name Larson from her mother's side of the family.

1996   Brie tells her mother that she really wants to be an actor. She begins taking lessons.

1997   Brie, her mother, and her sister move to Los Angeles, California. Brie starts going to auditions. Her parents divorce.

1998   She appears on *The Tonight Show with Jay Leno*. It is her first appearance before a national audience.

2001   She earns her first starring role, playing the daughter in the TV show *Raising Dad*. The job ends after one year.

2005   Brie releases a pop music album and goes on tour. The album, called *Finally Out of P.E.*, sells poorly.

2006   She costars in *Hoot*, a movie about saving owls. It is her biggest movie part so far. The movie gets bad reviews and fails to make money.

2009   Larson lands another starring TV role, again playing a daughter. *United States of Tara* lasts three seasons. Afterward, she has a hard time finding work.

2012   *Short Term 12* is Larson's first starring role in a movie. It wins awards and gets good reviews. It does not make much money.

2015   Larson stars in *Room*. She will win an Academy Award for Best Actress for this performance.

2017   She directs *Unicorn Store*, starring Samuel L. Jackson. She stars in *Kong: Skull Island*.

2019   Larson stars in *Captain Marvel*—the first movie in the Marvel Cinematic Universe to star a woman. It will go on to earn over $1 billion worldwide. She also appears in *Avengers: Endgame*, which blows the top off the box office with $357 million in sales on its opening weekend.

SELECTED FILMOGRAPHY

2020	*Just Mercy*	**2008**	*Tanner Hall*
2019	*Avengers: Endgame*	**2007**	*The Beautiful Ordinary*, also
	Captain Marvel		known as *Remember the Daze*
2017	*Unicorn Store* (also Directs)	**2006**	*Hoot*
	Kong: Skull Island	**2004**	*13 Going on 30*
	The Glass Castle		*Sleepover*
2015	*Room*	**2003**	*Right on Track*
2013	*The Spectacular Now*	**2001–2002**	*Raising Dad* (TV Show)
	Short Term 12	**1999**	*Special Delivery*
2012	*21 Jump Street*	**1998**	*The Tonight Show with Jay Leno*
2009–2011	*United States of Tara* (TV Show)		(TV Show)

Chapter 1. The Right Role

1. Keegan, Rebecca. "Brie Larson Can't Save Womankind (But She's Doing Her Best)." *Hollywood Reporter*, February 13 2019.
2. Ibid.
3. Mosa, Marilyn. "*Right on Track*. (TV Brief)." *Hollywood Reporter*, March 21, 2003, p. 87.
4. Riley, Jenelle. "A *Room* of Her Own." *Variety*, October 1, 2015, p. 40.

Chapter 2. Struggle

1. Riley, Jenelle. "A *Room* of Her Own." *Variety*, October 1, 2015. p. 40.
2. Baldonado, Ann Marie. "Actress Brie Larson Finds Light Within the Darkness of *Room*." *Fresh Air*, NPR, November 9, 2015. https://www.npr.org/templates/transcript/transcript.php?storyId=452552851
3. Riley.
4. Sandell, Laurie. "Brie Larson's 20-Year Climb to Overnight Stardom." *The Hollywood Reporter*, January 20, 2016. https://www.hollywoodreporter.com/features/brie-larsons-20-year-climb-857011
5. Larson, Brie. "My Worst Audition." *The Tonight Show with Jimmy Fallon* (web series), December 22, 2014. http://youtu.be/WNGH7WVnPmw

Chapter 4. Attention!

1. Bettinger, Brendan. "Brie Larson *21 Jump Street* Set Visit Interview." *Collider*, February 15, 2012. http://collider.com/brie-laron-21-jump-street-interview/
2. Ibid.
3. "Audience Scores for *21 Jump Street*,"Rottentomatoes.com. https://www.rottentomatoes.com/m/21_jump_street_2011
4. Riley, Jenelle. "A *Room* of Her Own." *Variety*, October 1, 2015. p. 40.
5. Baldonado, Ann Marie. "Actress Brie Larson Finds Light Within the Darkness of *Room*." *Fresh Air*. NPR, November 9, 2015. https://www.npr.org/templates/transcript/transcript.php?storyId=452552851
6. Riley.

Chapter 5. Fame

1. Sandell, Laurie. "Brie Larson's 20-Year Climb to Overnight Stardom." *The Hollywood Reporter*, January 20, 2016. https://www.hollywoodreporter.com/features/brie-larsons-20-year-climb-857011
2. "*Captain Marvel* Star Brie Larson Shares Intense Training for Superhero Role." *Sunday Today*, March 10, 2019. http://youtu.be/I8JfEpwbRME
3. "*Black Panther* Box Office," boxofficemojo.com https://www.boxofficemojo.com/movies/?id=marvel2017b.htm
4. Keegan, Rebecca. "Brie Larson Can't Save Womankind (But She's Doing Her Best)." *Hollywood Reporter*, February 13 2019./
5. Itzkoff, Dave. "At Marvel, a Female Superhero Gets to Shine." *The New York Times*, March 3, 2019, p. 12(L).

Books

Kimmel, Mike. *Acting Scenes for Kids and Tweens*. New York–New Orleans: Ben Rose Creative Arts, 2017.

On the Internet

Brie Larson: *Finally Out of P.E.*—AOL Sessions
https://m.youtube.com/watch?v=2X5EzzrdElk
Captain Marvel Official Site
https://www.marvel.com/movies/captain-marvel
Internet Movie Database: Brie Lawson
https://www.imdb.com/name/nm0488953/
Instagram
https://www.instagram.com/brielarson/?hl=en
Twitter
https://mobile.twitter.com/brielarson?lang=en

Works Consulted

Andreeva, Nellie. "Larson Is Latest *Tara* Personality." *Hollywood Reporter*, July 9, 2008.

"Audience Scores for *21 Jump Street*," Rottentomatoes.com. https://www.rottentomatoes.com/m/21_jump_street_2011

Baldonado, Ann Marie. "Actress Brie Larson Finds Light Within the Darkness of *Room*." *Fresh Air*, NPR, November 9, 2015. https://www.npr.org/templates/transcript/transcript.php?storyId=452552851

Bettinger, Brendan. "Brie Larson *21 Jump Street* Set Visit Interview." *Collider*, February 15, 2012. http://collider.com/brie-laron-21-jump-street-interview/

"*Black Panther* Box Office." *Box Office Mojo*. https://www.boxofficemojo.com/movies/?id=marvel2017b.htm

"Brie Larson Wins Best Actress." Academy Awards. March 23, 2016. " http://youtu.be/b_lq5wORkYA

Buckley, Cara. "When She Became the Target, the Rules Changed." *New York Times*, March 1, 2019.

"*Captain Marvel* Star Brie Larson Shares Intense Training for Superhero Role." *Sunday Today*, March 10, 2019. http://youtu.be/I8JfEpwbRME

Debruge, Peter. "Don Jon's Addiction." *Variety*, January 28, 2013.

Debruge, Peter. "'Short Term' Resonance." *Variety*, March 1, 2013.

Fabrizio,Tony. "Remember *Right on Track*? The Enders Sisters Are Still Formidable." ESPN.com, August 14, 2015. http://www.espn.com/espnw/news-commentary/article/13437473/remember-right-track-enders-sisters-formidable

Fallon, Jimmy. "Brie Larson's Career Kicked Off with a Sketch with Jay Leno." *The Tonight Show with Jimmy Fallon*, August 10, 2017. http://youtu.be/DjyQZ1GP5Gw

Gardner, Chris. "MGM Planning a *Sleepover* Party for Vega." *Hollywood Reporter*, September 17, 2003.

Itzkoff, Dave. "At Marvel, a Female Superhero Gets to Shine." *New York Times*, March 3, 2019.

Keegan, Rebecca. "Brie Larson Can't Save Womankind (But She's Doing Her Best)." *Hollywood Reporter*, February 13 2019.

Kit, Borys. "Brie Larson, Alexa Vega, Khleo Thomas, and Sean Marquette Are Shooting *The Beautiful Ordinary*." *Hollywood Reporter*. June 14, 2006.

"Wilson, Larson Give a Hoot for NL Family Film." *Hollywood Reporter*, June 28, 2005.

Lane, Anthony. "Shape-Shifters." *The New Yorker*, March 18, 2019.

Larson, Brie. "My Worst Audition." *The Tonight Show with Jimmy Fallon* (web series). December 22, 2014. http://youtu.be/WNGH7WVnPmw

MacAtee, Rebecca. "Ready to Launch: Inside Britney Spears, Justin Timberlake, Christina Aguilera & Ryan Gosling's Darling *Mickey Mouse Club* Days." *E Online*, September 19, 2018. https://www.eonline.com/news/969444/ready-to-launch-inside-britney-spears-justin-timberlake-christina-aguilera-ryan-gosling-s-darling-mickey-mouse-club-days

Mallenbaum, Carly. "Inclusion Strategies Have Sprung Up, but How to Really Move the Needle." *USA Today*, February, 28, 2019.

Mosa, Marilyn. "*Right on Track*. (TV Brief)," *Hollywood Reporter*, March 21, 2003.

Nelson, Rob. "*The Spectacular Now.*" *Variety*, January 28, 2013.

Oleszczyk, Michat. "*Room.*" *Cineaste*, Summer 2016.

Powers, John, and Valerie Steiker. "Free Spirit." *Vogue*, October, 2015.

Riley, Jenelle. "A *Room* of Her Own." *Variety*. October 1, 2015.

Ross, Deborah. "Mad about the Boy." *Spectator*, January 9, 2016.

Ross, Deborah. "Now, That's Better." *Spectator*, March 9, 2019.

Sandell, Laurie. "Brie Larson's 20-Year Climb to Overnight Stardom." *The Hollywood Reporter*, January 20, 2016. https://www.hollywoodreporter.com/features/brie-larsons-20-year-climb-857011

Sun, Rebecca. "'It's a Very Simple Formula to Create Change." *Hollywood Reporter*, December 5, 2018.

"Variety's 10 Actors to Watch Panel." *Variety*. October 15, 2013.

Zeitchik, Steven. "*Captain Marvel*: How the Trolls always Win—Until They Don't." *Washington Post*. March 7, 2019.

Zilberman, Alan. "'The Dark Knight' and Heath Ledger's Joker Were a Prescient Example of Troll Culture." *Washington Post*, July 13, 2018.

GLOSSARY

audition (aw-DIH-shun)—An actor's interview and tryout for a role.

casting director (KAS-ting dih-REK-ter)—A person who helps find actors for specific roles in a movie or TV show.

chiropractor (KY-roh-prak-ter)—A person who heals others by moving the joints of the body.

cinematic (sih-neh-MAA-tik)—Relating to movies.

commercial (kuh-MER-shul)—An ad that airs on TV or radio.

kidnap—To take a person against his or her will.

monologue (MAH-nuh-log)—A long speech by one actor.